Me and My Captain

Me and My Captain

Story and Pictures by

M. B. GOFFSTEIN

Farrar / Straus / Giroux / New York

To Diane Wolkstein

Me and My Captain

There is a fishing boat anchored
on the window sill below my shelf,

and I smell a briny smell
coming from it.

Looking down at its white cabin
with the green-painted roof
and gay red-colored flag,

I dream of her captain

somehow coming up to see me.

He would notice at once
that I have a ship in a bottle
and a collection of sea shells,

and ask me to marry him.

Then I would invite him
to stay for dinner.

One good thing about being a doll
is the food.

It is made out of plaster
and appetizingly painted,

so unless it gets too chipped or dusty
or left in the sunlight to fade,
it remains fresh-looking forever—

a feast for the eye.

If I were to serve the captain
with some,
and set the table with my Bristol dishes
and silver salt and pepper shakers,

he would really be amazed
at his good luck!

"Salt?" I would offer him.

"What? An old salt like me?"
he would say back.
And I would laugh and laugh.

He would feed my dog scraps of food
under the table,
and we three would be so cozy together.

Since the captain of a fishing boat
is often gone on long voyages,

my dog and I would stay here,
and our life would be just the same
as before.

But we would have someone to watch for
and wait for
and hope for good weather for.

And whatever happened
while he was away

would be something to tell him about
when he returned.

Even without knowing him,
when I look down at the captain's boat
on the window sill,

I feel happy because he is there.